# CLOUDS AND PRECIPITATION

**ELIZABETH KRAJNIK**

**PowerKiDS**
press.

NEW YORK

Published in 2019 by The Rosen Publishing Group, Inc.
29 East 21st Street, New York, NY 10010

Editor: Rachel Gintner
Cover Design: Michael Flynn
Interior Layout: Rachel Rising

Photo Credits: Cover Pictureguy/Shutterstock.com; Cover, pp. 3, 4, 6, 8, 9, 10, 12, 13, 14, 16, 17, 18, 19, 20, 21, 22, 23, 24 chaowat kawera/Shutterstock.com; pp. 5, 13, 15 Courtesy of NASA Image and Video Library; p. 7 trgrowth/Shutterstock.com; p. 8 The Washington Post/Contributor/Getty Images; p. 9 Martchan/Shutterstock.com; p. 11 MonoLiza/Shutterstock.com; p. 12 Barbara Barbour/Shutterstock.com; p. 16 michelmond/Shutterstock.com; p. 17 MitjaM/Shutterstock.com; p. 18 frantic00/Shutterstock.com; p. 19 SAIDU BAH/AFP/Getty Images; p. 20 Cammie Czuchnicki/Shutterstock.com; p. 21 Designua/Shutterstock.com; p. 22 Jeka/Shutterstock.com.

Cataloging-in-Publication Data

Names: Krajnik, Elizabeth.
Title: Clouds and precipitation / Elizabeth Krajnik.
Description: New York : PowerKids Press, 2019. | Series: Spotlight on weather and natural disasters | Includes glossary and index.
Identifiers: LCCN ISBN 9781508168881 (pbk.) | ISBN 9781508168867 (library bound) | ISBN 9781508168898 (6 pack)
Subjects: LCSH: Clouds--Juvenile literature. | Precipitation (Meteorology)--Juvenile literature.
Classification: LCC QC921.35 K73 2019 | DDC 551.57'6--dc23

Manufactured in the United States of America

CPSIA Compliance Information: Batch #CS18PK For further information contact Rosen Publishing, New York, New York at 1-800-237-9932.

# CONTENTS

# CHAPTER ONE

# PART OF EARTH'S SYSTEMS

Earth is made up of four systems that work together: the atmosphere, hydrosphere, geosphere, and biosphere. Clouds and **precipitation** are special because they're part of both the atmosphere and the hydrosphere. The atmosphere is the layer of gases surrounding Earth. The hydrosphere is the total amount of water on Earth.

Without clouds and precipitation, our planet would be very dry and wouldn't be able to support life. Clouds keep Earth warm at night and cool during the day. NASA studies clouds to better understand Earth's weather, or the daily state of the atmosphere. They also study the Earth's climate, or the average weather conditions over a period of years.

This book will talk about the different types of clouds, the types of precipitation they produce, and the natural **disasters** that can occur with or after increased precipitation.

A number of natural disasters are connected to clouds and precipitation. NASA uses **satellites** to study clouds from outer space and track weather patterns.

# CHAPTER TWO

# WHAT ARE CLOUDS?

Clouds are made of water drops or ice crystals that are light enough to float in the sky. They form when water changes into water vapor, the gaseous state of water. This process is called evaporation. When the water vapor rises high enough in the sky, the temperature of the atmosphere drops, causing the water vapor to cool. The water vapor condenses, or changes from a gas to a liquid, and forms water droplets. These droplets stick to **particles** floating in the air, such as dust, ice, or salt from Earth's oceans. This creates a cloud.

Clouds also begin to form when air that has warmed near the Earth's surface rises into the atmosphere. Air rises because it's lighter and less dense, or tightly packed, when warm. Once the air reaches a certain **altitude**, the lower temperature and air pressure cause water vapor to condense, creating a cloud.

# THE WATER CYCLE

**CONDENSATION**

**EVAPORATION**

**PRECIPITATION**

**RUNOFF**

Clouds are formed as part of the water **cycle**. The water cycle is the movement of water from the hydrosphere to the atmosphere and back.

# CHAPTER THREE

# CLOUD TYPES

Because clouds form in a number of ways, there are many different types of clouds. Clouds get their names from their shape and where they're found in the sky. Clouds that form high in the atmosphere include cirrocumulus, cirrus, and cirrostratus clouds. Clouds that form in the middle include altocumulus and altostratus clouds. Low clouds include stratus, cumulus, and stratocumulus clouds.

*Cumulonimbus* is the Latin word meaning "column rain." Even though these clouds can be nice to look at, they can produce heavy precipitation, lightning, strong winds, and even tornadoes.

CIRRUS CLOUDS

Clouds that have "cirro" or "cirrus" in their name are wispy, almost like feathers. *Cirrus* means "curl" in Latin. These clouds form between 16,500 and 45,000 feet (5,029.2 and 13,716 m) high in the atmosphere. Clouds with the Latin *cumulus* in their name are fluffy and form in different layers of the atmosphere. *Cumulus* means "heap" in Latin. Clouds with "strato" or "stratus" in their name form in different layers of the atmosphere. *Stratus* means "layer" in Latin.

# CHAPTER FOUR

# MAKING IT RAIN

Many clouds produce precipitation. The most common types of precipitation are rain, hail, and snow. However, there are other types of precipitation, such as sleet. Sleet is rain that falls from clouds but freezes before it reaches the ground.

Most clouds that produce rain and snow have "nimbo" or "nimbus" in their name. For example, nimbostratus clouds produce precipitation that can last for many hours. They are low-atmosphere clouds that are full of moisture. Cumulonimbus clouds produce rain, thunder, and lightning. Lightning is produced when positively charged particles and negatively charged particles are separated. This forms an electrical field, which, when strong enough, will let loose a bolt of lightning.

**Global warming** can also affect global precipitation. As the earth warms, ice in the atmosphere evaporates. It becomes water vapor that condenses into precipitation.

If you hear thunder or see lightning, be sure to go inside.
Storms can be unsafe!

# CHAPTER FIVE

# SCARY SNOWSTORMS

Snow can be beautiful, but snowstorms can be scary. Nimbostratus and cumulonimbus clouds most often produce snow. For snow to form, the temperature of the air must remain at or below the temperature at which water freezes, which is 32°Fahrenheit (0°Celsius), throughout the atmosphere.

Snow flurries are instances of light snow that fall for just a short while. However, different kinds of snowstorms can create problems for people.

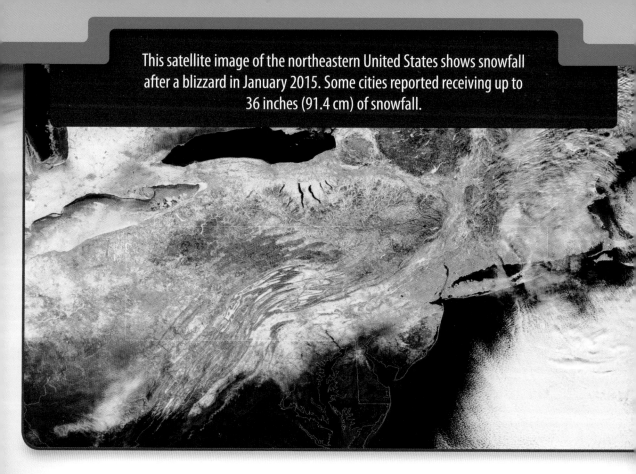

This satellite image of the northeastern United States shows snowfall after a blizzard in January 2015. Some cities reported receiving up to 36 inches (91.4 cm) of snowfall.

Blizzards are snowstorms that occur when winds are blowing at speeds of more than 35 miles (56.3 km) per hour. The wind blows snow and creates poor visibility of 0.25 miles (0.4 km) or less for more than three hours.

People living in regions where snow is common need to be prepared for blizzards and other winter weather. One of the easiest ways to stay safe during a blizzard or in **extreme** cold is to stay inside.

# CHAPTER SIX

# HORRIBLE HURRICANES

A hurricane is a **tropical** cyclone, or rotating storm, with winds that are moving at 74 miles (119.1 km) per hour or more. Winds this strong can do a lot of **damage** to buildings and trees. Hurricanes form over tropical oceans and sometimes strike land. They're called typhoons when they form over the northwest Pacific Ocean or the China Sea. Hurricane season in the Atlantic Ocean runs from June 1 to November 30 and the eastern Pacific hurricane season runs from May 15 to November 30.

If a hurricane reaches land, it can cause a storm surge. This is a wall of ocean water that the storm pushes ashore. Hurricanes also include heavy rain. Together, these things can cause flooding. Rain bands are areas of clouds and rain surrounding a hurricane's center. These can stretch for hundreds of miles. The hurricane's center is also called the hurricane's eye.

On September 14, 2014, Hurricane Odile struck land near Cabo San Lucas, Mexico. This was a Category 3 hurricane, meaning it had winds of 111 to 129 miles (178.6 to 207.6 km) per hour. Heavy rainfall came one week after the hurricane touched ground.

# CHAPTER SEVEN

# FIERCE FLOODS

Floods are some of the deadliest and most harmful natural disasters on Earth. Flooding occurs when land that is usually dry is covered with water. This can happen when a lot of rain falls or when a lot of snow melts quickly. Floods can also happen if dams fail.

A flood warning means that a flood is happening or will happen very soon. This means you and your family should get to high ground as quickly as you can. One foot (0.3 m) of moving water can sweep your car away.

Most flooding happens over a period of hours or days, giving people living in at-risk areas time to evacuate, or leave. However, flash floods give little to no warning, making it very challenging for people to prepare. Flash floods can quickly sweep away objects in their path, such as cars and houses.

Floods are so **dangerous** because they're hard to see coming. It can be hard to tell which areas will be affected by a flood. If people aren't prepared, structures that aren't built to survive floods may be swept away.

# CHAPTER EIGHT

# MUDSLIDE MADNESS

Heavy rains can cause more than just flooding. Mudslides can also occur after heavy rains or when snow melts very quickly. A mudslide is moving rock, earth, and other wet **debris**. This flows down a slope, gains speed, and often grows as it tears trees and other objects out of the ground. Mudslides can also collect large rocks and cars. They can even move houses.

Mudslides can kill hundreds and leave hundreds more homeless in just a few short moments. It's more likely for mudslides to happen in areas that have been deforested, where many trees and forests have been cut down and the land is cleared.

Mudslides can happen almost anywhere. They are also very tricky to see coming and can strike at any moment. Unlike other natural disasters, mudslides aren't always related to storms and large amounts of precipitation. Human activities, such as construction or land clearing, can weaken the ground and cause land formations to loosen. The earth in the open areas created by these activities can become full of water more easily than earth in protected areas.

# CHAPTER NINE

# TERRIBLE TORNADOES

A tornado is a powerful whirling wind with a cloud that is shaped like a funnel. It moves over land in a narrow path. The funnel stretches between the clouds of a thunderstorm (usually cumulonimbus clouds) and the ground. Tornadoes are the most severe atmospheric storms on Earth.

Supercells, or large, rotating thunderstorms, are more likely to produce tornadoes. However, not all tornadoes are produced by supercells.

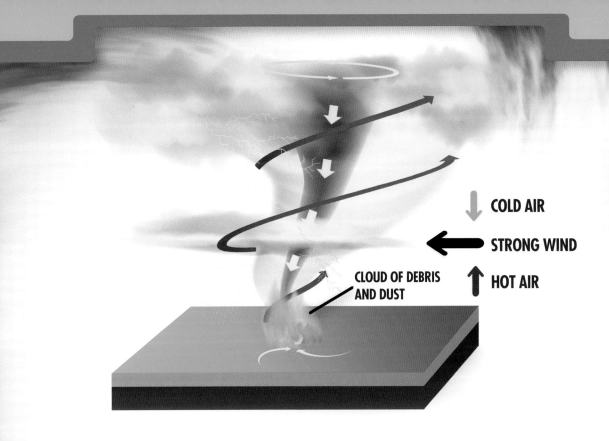

COLD AIR

STRONG WIND

CLOUD OF DEBRIS
AND DUST

HOT AIR

In the United States, tornadoes form when warm, moist air from the south and cold, dry air from the north meet. The warm air slips under the cold air and then rises, creating a **horizontal**, spinning tube of air. The air nearest the ground, warmed by the sun, begins to lift the middle part of the spinning tube. This forms two **vertical** rotating tubes of air, the weaker of which dies off. The stronger of the two spinning tubes becomes the heart of the thunderstorm. From here, a **mesocyclone** may form, which allows the storm to continue growing.

# CHAPTER TEN

# KEEP YOURSELF SAFE

Clouds and precipitation are important parts of Earth's systems. Clouds keep Earth warm at night and cool during the day. They form the precipitation necessary to water our crops and provide humans and animals with drinking water.

You should always be aware of what the weather is doing. If the clouds in the sky change quickly, that might mean bad weather is on its way. Sometimes, when a tornado is forming, the sky will turn a very dark green color. Move inside if it begins to hail, if you see lightning, or if you hear thunder.

If you live in an area where blizzards, flooding, or tornadoes are common, be on the lookout for these types of weather patterns. Weather experts in your area will be sure to keep you informed of any possible storms.

# GLOSSARY

**altitude (AL-tuh-tood)** The height of something above a certain level.

**cycle (SY-kuhl)** A series of events that, once complete, repeats itself.

**damage (DAA-mij)** Loss or harm done to a person or an object.

**dangerous (DAYN-juh-ruhs)** Not safe.

**debris (duh-BREE)** Broken pieces of objects or objects left somewhere.

**disaster (dih-ZAS-tur)** An event that happens suddenly and causes much suffering and loss, often for many people.

**extreme (ihk-STREEM)** Very great in degree.

**global warming (GLOH-buhl WAHR-ming)** The rise in temperature of Earth's atmosphere and oceans that is thought to occur, in part, because of air pollution.

**horizontal (hor-uh-ZAHN-tuhl)** Positioned from side to side rather than up and down.

**mesocyclone (meh-zoh-SY-klohn)** A quickly rotating section of air within a thunderstorm that often creates a tornado.

**particle (PAR-tih-kuhl)** A very small piece of something; also, any one of the smallest parts of matter.

**precipitation (prih-sih-puh-TAY-shun)** Water that falls to the earth as hail, mist, rain, sleet, or snow.

**satellite (SAA-tuh-lyt)** A spacecraft placed in orbit around Earth, a moon, or a planet to collect information or for communication.

**tropical (TRAH-pih-kuhl)** Of or relating to the tropics, usually having to do with warm, wet weather.

**vertical (VUHR-tih-kuhl)** Positioned up and down rather than from side to side.

# INDEX

# PRIMARY SOURCE LIST

**Page 5**
Blue Marble Earth montage. Satellite image. Created by NASA. January 30, 2012. Courtesy of NASA.

**Page 13**
Post-storm snowfall in northeastern United States. Satellite image. Created by NASA. January 28, 2015. Courtesy of NASA.

**Page 15**
Hurricane Odile, Cabo San Lucas, Mexico. Satellite image. Created by NASA. September 14, 2014. Courtesy of NASA.

# WEBSITES

Due to the changing nature of Internet links, PowerKids Press has developed an online list of websites related to the subject of this book. This site is updated regularly. Please use this link to access the list: www.powerkidslinks.com/swnd/precip